The Boy

who wanted to be a

Mouse

An inspiring true story of an African child.

Written by Esther Osazee Itamah

Illustrated by Emem Essien

This Book Belongs to

____

First published in London 2023

Text copyright © Esther Osazee Itamah

Illustrations copyright ® Emem Essien

All rights reserved.

No part of this publication may be reproduced, or transmitted in any form, or by any means, electrical, mechanical, photocopying, recording or otherwise without the written permission of the publishers.

ISBN

ISBN 978-1-3999-5930-8

Dedication

This book is specially dedicated to Vasil and Vernice—for being strong, resilient, unbreakable, intelligent, and knowing who you are despite the odds and opinions of others. It is also for all African children out there in an unfamiliar ground trying to find their feet. You are enough, you are beautiful, you are special and a masterpiece. Walk with your shoulders high, for you are not a Mouse.

Background

Moving to another country takes a toll, and it does so exceptionally for many young minds like my nearly four-year-old son at the time of this event. Such children are pulled away from all they have known: friends, extended family members, culture, and their way of life. They must survive in a new environment where sometimes their very existence, the way they speak, their skin colour and hair type, and even the food they eat are questioned. And these questions come not from genuine interest or mere curiosity, but from a place of suspicion and disdain. They are despised for it.

The Boy Who Wanted to Be a Mouse is a story based on my son as he sought the best way to handle the harsh reality of his new and unreceptive environment. Looking through his eyes, we can understand the 'Why' behind his resolve.

Background

It is also an in-depth story of children taken by their parents from familiar grounds to endure a hostile environment. Some parents come to study or attain more education. They are immigrants who, for fear of their unstable societies, believe in the dream of providing a better life for their kids. These refugees and asylum seekers face dangers that threaten their lives and very existence. They seek refuge, opportunities, and homes elsewhere. There are also expatriates and professionals, like doctors, nurses, caregivers, teachers and IT specialists, all from different walks of life.

This story depicts a personal encounter of children believed to be of another race. I use the word 'believed' intentionally, because I do not believe or accept the word 'race' as a term of differentiating people. If I am to quote the respectable singer Innocent Idibia (popularly known as Two Baba), "There is only one race, and that is the human race."

Background

The Boy Who Wanted to Be a Mouse is prompted and created from the emotional trauma, discrimination, and cultural shock some children experience not only from their peers but from adults alike . This can even include those they respect and trust, ranging from teachers and parents to neighbors, etc.

This picture book opens our minds to see that whilst this set of parents struggle to adjust in their new environments, some children fight their own silent battles. It may seem they do not, because they struggle to understand and articulate their new experience.

This story is not intended to sadden young readers or make them feel dejected, but rather to encourage them and inspire them to build communal spirits among kids from all backgrounds. The core theme of this book urges kids to treat individuals the way they want to be treated. The story can be independently read by children ages 7-9, and for ages 4-6 with the help of a parent or teacher.

"Aaaah!" a distant, panicked scream roared.
The echoes rang throughout the house like
the faint clang of a bell.

It was Gosa's sister Efe and her acute fear of a Mouse. Their mother had come to the rescue, but Gosa stood far off. He had questions to ask about the Mouse's frequent visits to their kitchen.

"Iye," he said to his mother, "how does a Mouse get into people's homes?" His ever-curious mind was always looking for something new. Gosa's family had recently moved from Nigeria to Scotland, which was an enormous change. More than ever, he had questions about his new environment.

"A Mouse sometimes enter homes because it smells food, and then it sees an accessible point of entry."
"Aha..." Gosa gasped.
"Yes," his mother affirmed.
"Does that mean they are here just for food, Iye?" Gosa asked.
His questioning, dark-brown eyes watched her as he waited earnestly for an answer.
"Food and shelter," his mother replied.
"Oh, dear poor Mouse."
A frown deepened on his little narrow face. He honestly felt sorry and sad. His sister always screamed when she saw a Mouse, and their mother would throw it outside. However, the poor Mouse was only here for food and shelter.
"So why do we fear and chase them out?" His tiny fingers pulled a braid of hair that fell across his face. His mother could tell he was eager to understand.

His mother leaned against the wall to gather her thoughts, knowing this would be one of Gosa's many questioning sessions.
"Mice are more afraid of humans than humans are of them, so they try to stay hidden and draw no attention to themselves. They can be very quiet and compliant, which means they agree, accept situations, and obey. Maybe a bit too much. But, they do it so they can remain unnoticed and tolerated. And in a Mouse's case with humans, they are not to be seen and heard, especially in human homes like in our kitchen." She added the last bit with a smile. His mother walked away, leaving Gosa completely dazed and with a new resolution in his tiny mind.

Faster, faster!
Run along, Gosa.
Your Sister is way ahead.
But why the gloom? You always loved school.
Gosa reluctantly trudged behind and muttered.
"Not this one, and not in this place."

He took a few quick steps to catch up with his mother
and sister. Gosa had been thinking last night about his
mother's explanation of the Mouse and how it survived.
Now, he had to do the same in his new school where
he and his sister were the only ones like them.
"Iye, if I keep quiet and compl..."
"Compliant you mean, Gosa."
"Yes, that word...like the Mouse does, would that make
me have friends and be liked?"
"Stop being silly, Gosa. You are liked, and you will make
friends soon. You just need to give your new classmates
time to adjust."

Gosa sat alone at his desk because Miss Milles, the class teacher, brought out plain sheets and crayons for their class activity.
Gosa would usually run alongside his classmates to pick his favorite colour of crayon before it was taken by another, but he sat back and allowed them to have a go before picking whichever was left.

At least this way, they won't pull away from me, he thought in his tiny mind.
Like the Mouse, he was going to be quiet and compliant.
A B C D E F G
H I J K L M N
O P Q R S T U
V W X Y Z

And when the time came for their exercise activity, Miss Milles asked the pupils to form a circle holding hands. But like several times before, no one held Gosa's hand from either side.
He would usually reach for their hands, and although they refused to touch him, he would insist until Miss Milles told him to partake in the exercise without his hands being held.

Like the Mouse, he would agree and accept situations like this. He listened to Miss Milles' frequent advice in such matters, and he told himself that they would come around.

ABCDEFG
HIJKLMN
OPQRSTU
VWXYZ

The pupils were at the playground during their break, some picking wildflowers and building sandcastles, while others were running around with friends in hot pursuit. Gosa shielded himself behind an old dollhouse at the far end of the play area where the sun cast a shadow of the big oak tree over the fence. Gosa would usually join his classmates in hide-and-seek, but he decided he would be here, since it was better than being told the game wasn't for people like him. He believed they were right; he was the only one like him in his class. Brown skin, coarse thick hair, dark brown eyeballs, and he spoke and sounded different from them too.
Like the Mouse, he would stay hidden and draw no attention to himself.

It's been many weeks of Gosa playing a Mouse, and he's as disappointed as when he had first made his decision. It did not make the difference he hoped it would. It did not make any of his classmates bring him his favorite crayon colour when he did not join them although he had done it for some of them in his helpful spirit.

Sitting still by his desk, feeling more alone than he ever did, what was he to do? Being a Mouse did not make him more friends, for he felt invisible. He must've been missing something. Perhaps he should ask his Iye why it worked for the Mouse and not him. But deep within, Gosa's mind was changing. He would speak to his Iye and that would help him decide whether or not to try something different.

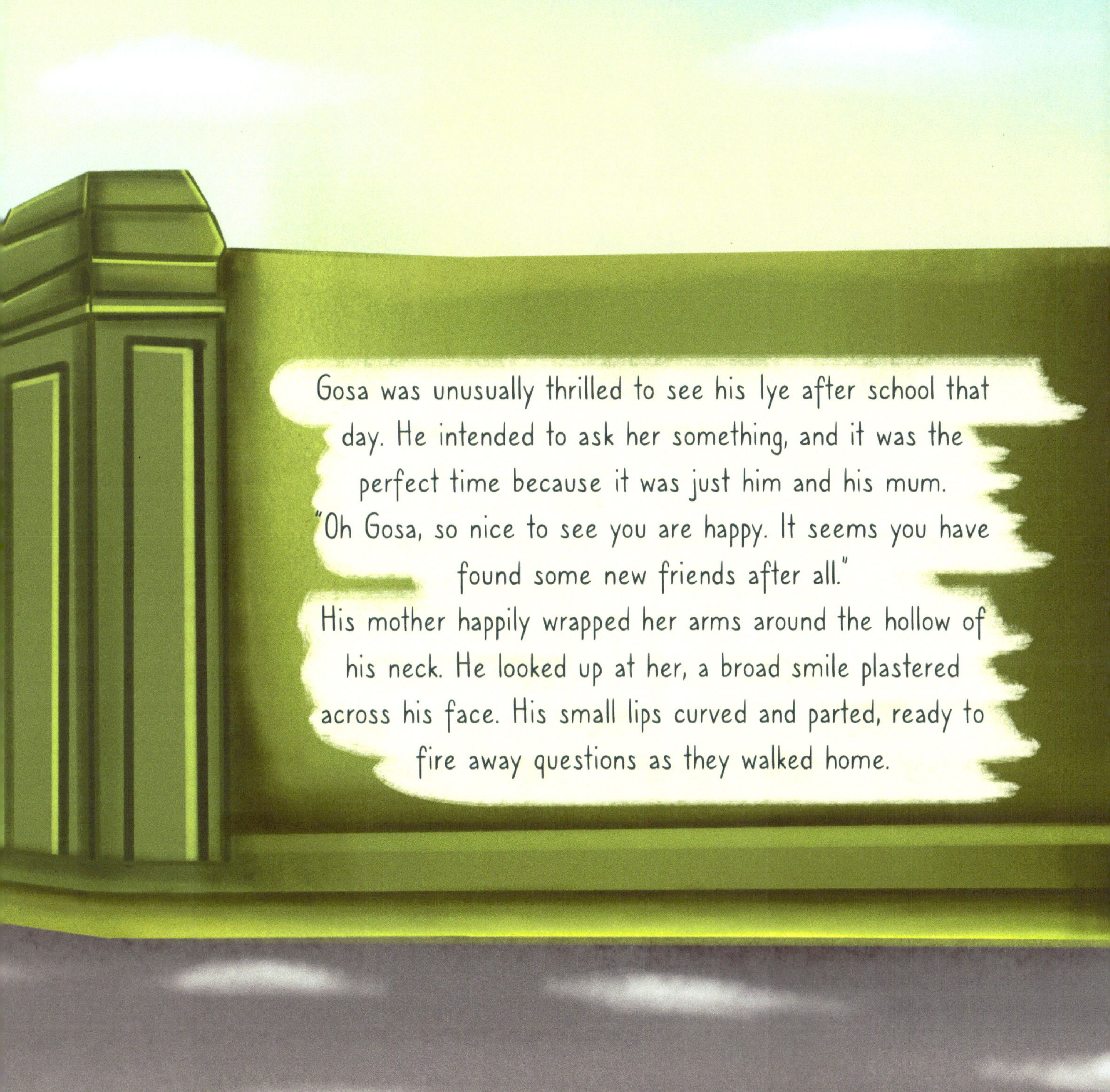

Gosa was unusually thrilled to see his Iye after school that
day. He intended to ask her something, and it was the
perfect time because it was just him and his mum.
"Oh Gosa, so nice to see you are happy. It seems you have
found some new friends after all."
His mother happily wrapped her arms around the hollow of
his neck. He looked up at her, a broad smile plastered
across his face. His small lips curved and parted, ready to
fire away questions as they walked home.

"Iye, I want to know more about the Mouse."
"You have gotten quite fond of the Mouse of late, Gosa."
He looked at his mother, his radiant eyes hoping for her approval,
but he was determined to get his answers. So, he carried on.
"Since the Mouse obeys, stays quiet and compl..."
"Compliant," she added, smiling.
"Yes, that is the word, Iye. Thank you."
"You're welcome, Gosa. Continue with your question. I would love to
hear what you have to say."
"Did it make people accept the Mouse?"

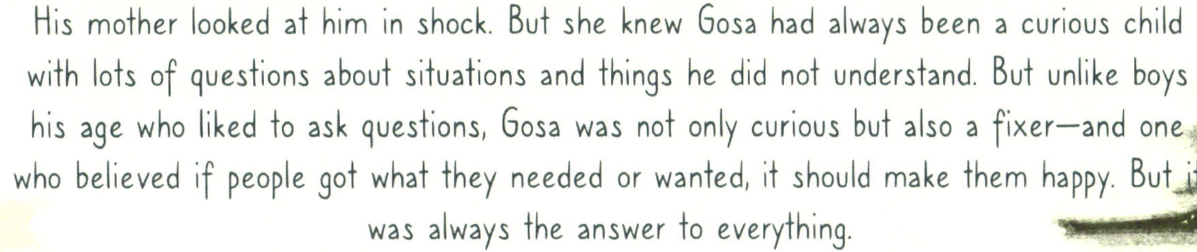

His mother looked at him in shock. But she knew Gosa had always been a curious child with lots of questions about situations and things he did not understand. But unlike boys his age who liked to ask questions, Gosa was not only curious but also a fixer—and one who believed if people got what they needed or wanted, it should make them happy. But it was always the answer to everything.

"Yes and no. Mice are animals, and although they might be compliant, hidden, unnoticed, ignored and quiet as much as they try to be, it is inevitable how they're seen by humans, and that may never change. Take for instance the mouse in our kitchen last night. Would you be comfortable with your mouse in our kitchen if it wasn't your pet?"

Gosa nodded in response.

"I guessed your answer would be no. The same applies to others. However, if the Mouse were aware that it didn't need to suppress itself at all, it would..."

"What does suppress mean, Iye?"
"I knew you would ask."
They both smiled.
"It means to restrain."
Looking at the expression on his face, she knew he didn't get it. His eyes
widened and he shrugged as he raised his hand.
"Suppress means to stop oneself from expressing their true feelings."
"Aha...I know that feeling, Iye."
Of course he did, and he had been experiencing it for a while now. He felt it
whenever he wanted to join his classmates to run for the crayons, or during
the exercise where they held hands, and at the play area for hide-and-seek.
He was all too familiar with suppression.
"Good," his mother said. " So, if the Mouse knew it didn't need to suppress
itself and be invisible, but instead realized that like with all living things
created, there was a special place for everyone, whether human or Mouse,
then it would be better for it."
Gosa's eyes lit up. He finally began to understand that suppressing how he felt
or who he was would only make him sad. Like his mother said, he had a
special place in the world, and accepting that would make him happy.
"Iye, then it seems to me that what will make me happy is being who I really
am and knowing that I have a purpose."
"Yes, Gosa."
Gosa understood more than his mother could anticipate. This reassured him in
his new decision, since his recent experiment had failed. He walked home a
happy boy that day, no longer burdened with trying to be a Mouse. He was just
going to be himself. It was the happiest his mother had seen him since he
started school there.

Gosa came to school the next morning happy and resolved that he was not going to shrink himself or be passive like a Mouse. He realized that as Gosa, he may not have friends, but he would make himself known, despite how his classmates would react. It did not matter if they pulled away from him when he happily went to get crayons, or when they refused to hold hands during their little exercise, or even when they were at the playground and told him their games were not for people like him.

Making himself visible and present was certainly better than being invisible and hidden. He was here, and he had a place and a purpose, like all people. He would be happy and refused to be reduced to a Mouse, for he was Gosa. As he sat at his desk smiling, he colored in a picture of a rainbow. He turned to see one of his classmates, who with a shy grin brought over an extra crayon for Gosa.

before scurrying back to his seat.

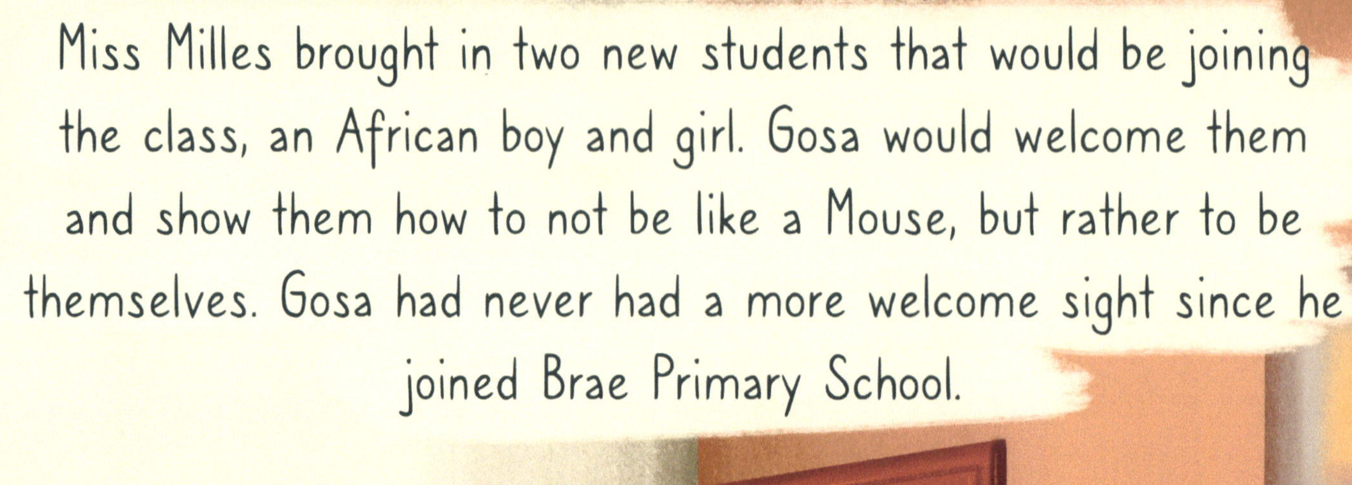

Miss Milles brought in two new students that would be joining the class, an African boy and girl. Gosa would welcome them and show them how to not be like a Mouse, but rather to be themselves. Gosa had never had a more welcome sight since he joined Brae Primary School.

Words and Meaning

Iye – Means Mother (It is a translation from the Bini language spoken by the Edo people of Nigeria)

THE END

www.ingramcontent.com/pod-product-compliance
Lightning Source LLC
Chambersburg PA
CBHW042155030726
47599CB00004B/742